tinder
nightmares

tinder nightmares

presented by unspirational
ABRAMS IMAGE, NEW YORK

Editor: Samantha Weiner
Designer: Devin Grosz
Production Manager: Anet Sirna-Bruder

Library of Congress Control Number: 2015940051

ISBN: 978-1-4197-1920-2

Printed and bound in the United States
10 9 8 7 6 5 4 3 2 1

Abrams Image books are available at special discounts when
purchased in quantity for premiums and promotions as well
as fundraising or educational use. Special editions can also
be created to specification. For details, contact specialsales@
abramsbooks.com or the address below.

THE ART OF BOOKS SINCE 1949
115 West 18th Street
New York, NY 10011
www.abramsbooks.com

contents

introduction

Happily ever after.

We are dropped onto this planet without an instruction manual. We aren't given a goal and told to reach it. All we have are our families, our friends, a flawed society, and a set of genitals that tell us what to do, for better or for worse.

With that in mind, we move through life looking for that perfect puzzle piece to complete us, and the older we get, the more we realize we're not one of those simple six-piece puzzles that we had as kids. We are complex, and finding the corresponding piece to help bring that picture together seems impossible.

So we go on dates, and we ask our friends if we know anyone who would like us, and we sit at bars alone and go home drunk and eat macaroni and cheese over a trash can and cry in the shower until the sun comes up.

And just when we start to think that we're so complicated we have to just give it all up, well, then we download Tinder. And we start swiping.

Every nope. Every yes. Every match. Every message. They're all little steps toward that happily ever after. But we're all bound to try one hundred wrong pieces before we find the one right piece that fits.

At first it's frustrating, trying over and over again to fit those ridges and curves in just the right places, but after a while, it just gets funny. And then, once you have abandoned all hope, once you feel like you're just going to live in a studio apartment with a giant pile of sad cats forever, you take one last shot in the dark and find that missing piece. And you look down and you realize that your picture is complete. Your happily ever after is right in front of you. You did it. Life. Completed.

This book is not about that.

This book is about all those shitty, misshaped, weird little puzzle pieces along the way. They're all part of the journey. They're gross and hilarious and weird and they make you wonder what the fuck is even going on. These are the people on the journey with you. And they're all really weird. So flip through these pages and laugh at the life you're living on the way to the life you want. And by the time you get to the end of this book, we hope you've found that happily ever after you've always wanted.

But if you don't, well, I guess it sucks to be you

pickup lines

How do you meet a person?
How do you get to know them
quickly? Well, an easy way is to
ask them a wildly inappropriate
question and see if they fall in
love with you. But chances are,
they'll just end up laughing at
you with their friends

MALCOLM   MAR 3 2015 7:13 PM

are you my appendix? because I don't understand how you work but this feeling in my stomach makes me want to take you out

✖ Surgery sounds like fun compared to dating you

DREW   FEB 25 2015 1:01 PM

Are you a campfire?

Cause you're hot and I want s'more. 😎

✖ Set yourself on fire

DAVE   FEB 25 2015 10:38 PM

You must be a small amount of red phosphorous and I must be a tiny stick because... we're a match.

✖ Guys, don't describe yourself as a tiny stick

KIRK　　　　　**MAR 1 2015 12:16 PM**

> Favorite non pornographic magazine to masturbate too?

 To*

HANK　　　　　**FEB 26 2015 9:15 PM**

> *insert witty pickup line in hopes of getting a response*

MAR 3 2015 11:14 PM

> Try harder

 Better luck next time, Hank

DENNIS　　　　　**JAN 1 2015 9:23 AM**

> Are you SATs? Cause Id do you for 3 hours and 45 minutes with snack breaks

 Why don't you skip the "doing" and just bring her some snacks?

LEE   FEB 21 2015 10:13 PM

I'd rock you like a 40 year old dad rocks a fanny pack at Disneyland

FEB 22 2015 10:00 AM

That's pretty hard
I like that

FEB 22 2015 11:30 AM

Just how I roll dawg

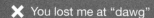 You lost me at "dawg"

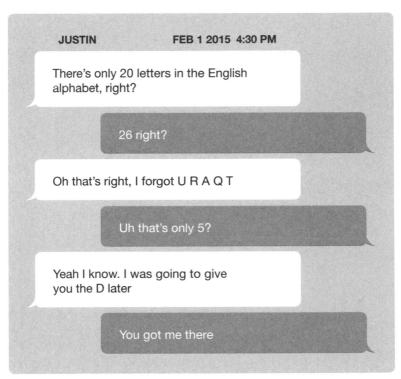

KATIE   FEB 28 2014 10:12 PM

Are you from Starbucks because I like you a latte

✖ I'll have a double espressNO

JUSTIN   FEB 1 2015 4:30 PM

There's only 20 letters in the English alphabet, right?

26 right?

Oh that's right, I forgot U R A Q T

Uh that's only 5?

Yeah I know. I was going to give you the D later

You got me there

✖ You forgot S T F U

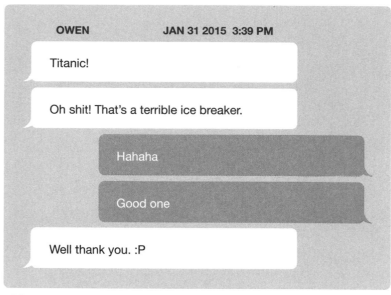

OWEN   JAN 31 2015 3:39 PM

Titanic!

Oh shit! That's a terrible ice breaker.

Hahaha

Good one

Well thank you. :P

✖ Too soon?

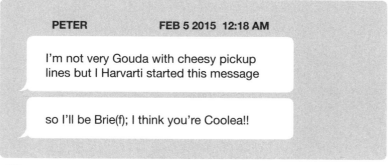

PETER   FEB 5 2015 12:18 AM

I'm not very Gouda with cheesy pickup lines but I Harvarti started this message

so I'll be Brie(f); I think you're Coolea!!

✖ This guy seems like a Muenster

AARON MAR 6 2015 7:18 AM

Knock knock

Who's there

Dewey

Dewey who?

Dewey have to wear a condom??

✗ Yes, Dewey. You definitely shouldn't be having kids

FREDDIE   FEB 23 2015 2:35 PM

You interested in a minute and a half of mediocre sex with the lights on? I'll take you to mcdonalds and split the check to prove I'm no weirdo

✖ I'm lovin' it

GERARD   FEB 2 2015 7:51 PM

are you a haunted house? cause i might cry after i come inside you

✖ Now I'm scared too

PATRICK   MAR 7 2015 3:36 PM

Yooooo

Having sex with me will make your night, but having anal sex with me will make your hole weak

✖ Ughhhhhhh

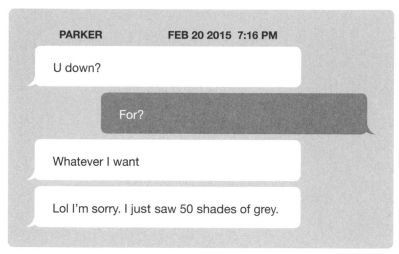

PARKER   FEB 20 2015 7:16 PM

U down?

For?

Whatever I want

Lol I'm sorry. I just saw 50 shades of grey.

✖ Did you just "LOL" at yourself?

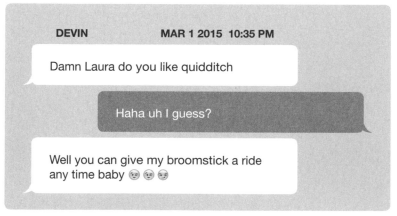

DEVIN   MAR 1 2015 10:35 PM

Damn Laura do you like quidditch

Haha uh I guess?

Well you can give my broomstick a ride any time baby 😉😉😉

✖ Harry Notter

Your parents will not like me. I will fall short of all your expectations. I will ruin your credit score.
But if you let me have sex with you I'll make you the happiest woman in the world for an entire night. Or 15 minutes. Actually probably more like 5

Haha well don't you sound like a keeper

✖ Ruining someone's credit score *is* a deal breaker

CLAY MAR 2 2015 3:09 PM

Are you Jewish? Cause you Isreali hot

 Oy vey

NATHANIEL MAR 6 2015 7:18 AM

My favorite holiday is thanksgiving...
how about you be the turkey and ill
do the stuffing?

Can't stand stuffing. Sorry kid

Are you gay

I think I am now

Why are you still talking

Do you want to see a picture of a
Burmese python?

 That was a bit of a leap, no?

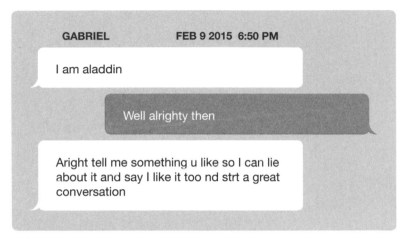

GABRIEL FEB 9 2015 6:50 PM

I am aladdin

Well alrighty then

Aright tell me something u like so I can lie about it and say I like it too nd strt a great conversation

✖ She won't be showing him *her* world

JESSE JAN 4 2015 9:32 PM

If you are feeling down, I can feel you up

✖ Can you feel that? It's the feeling of failure

LEO MAR 2 2015 3:59 AM

Hey can I read your shirt in braille?

✖ That's insensitive

DANNY   MAR 8 2015 10:23 PM

I want to treat you like my little toe and bang you all over my furniture.

And then cry a lot . . .

✘ I want to treat you like my whole foot and suffocate you with a sock

CHRIS   JAN 31 2015 9:39 PM

You can tell a lot about a woman by their ankles. For instance if she puts them by her ears she likes you.

✘ You can tell a lot by how fast a guy puts his foot in his mouth

OSCAR   MAR 5 2015 10:28 AM

If you were a vegetable you'd be a fineapple

✘ Well that's apPEARant

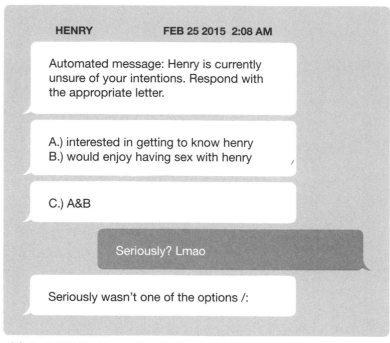

HENRY   **FEB 25 2015 2:08 AM**

Automated message: Henry is currently unsure of your intentions. Respond with the appropriate letter.

A.) interested in getting to know henry
B.) would enjoy having sex with henry

C.) A&B

Seriously? Lmao

Seriously wasn't one of the options /:

✖ D: The thing Henry won't be giving anyone anytime soon

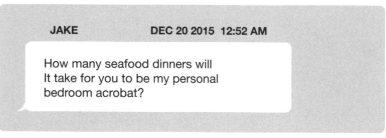

JAKE   **DEC 20 2015 12:52 AM**

How many seafood dinners will It take for you to be my personal bedroom acrobat?

✖ Do you really want her bouncing around after all that seafood?

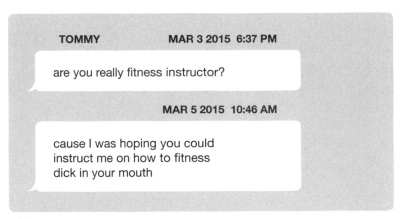

TOMMY 　　　　**MAR 3 2015 6:37 PM**

are you really fitness instructor?

MAR 5 2015 10:46 AM

cause I was hoping you could instruct me on how to fitness dick in your mouth

✖ "Are you really fitness instructor . . ."

APRIL 　　　　**FEB 3 2015 11:14 AM**

Hey matt, what are you up to?

Just waiting for the end of March so I can jump into you April 😊

Ahh, that's the best pickup line I've heard

Yeah I do work babe

✖ Take a long March off a short pier, pal

GEORGE   FEB 1 2015 4:12 PM

It's funny how when you get older you start to like the things you hated as a kid, like taking naps and getting spanked

✗ We should all go back to a simpler time

ANDREW   **JAN 6 2015 3:05 PM**

Want to come over to my place and watch porn on my flatscreen mirror?

✘ That's not how that works . . .

HAL   **FEB 21 2015 11:45 AM**

I would battle a pack of wild mountain lions inside a handicapped stall at McDonald's with my hands tied behind my back and a shake weight super glued to my forehead as my only weapon just to share a freshly baked pizza with you over Skype with a dial up connection

✘ Seems reasonable

JERRY   **MAR 4 2015 10:39 PM**

If you were a washing machine I would fill you with my dirty load

✘ Literally vomiting

GARY   DEC 22 2014 7:01 PM

Hey girl

You sitting on the F5 key?
Coz that ass is refreshing.

Don't say that again lol

Ok sorry

But in all seriousness, if I was a
taxidermist and your pet donkey died,
would you let me stuff that ass?

Ssshh

What's the point in being on here
if you're gona be a douche :/

Haha sorry. If you were a vegetable
you'd be a cutecumber :)

✖ How long can this go on for?

WAYNE　　　　FEB 24 2015 4:45 PM

Do you know karate

No...

Well then why is your body so kickin

✖ Nice try, Bruce Lee

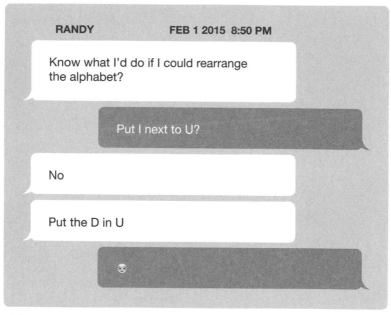

✖ Let's put the "F" before the "U"

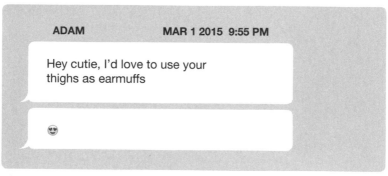

✖ I bet she'd crush your head like a melon

ISAAC   MAR 5 2015 6:44 PM

Damn girl, are you a can of pilsbury biscuits? Because I'd love to bang you on the counter until you bust.

✖ She'd probably rather get a yeast infection

OLIVER   JAN 31 2015 1:40 AM

Are you my appendix...

Because I hardly know you but you give me a feeling In my gut that I should take you out. ;)

✖ Again with this shit?

MARK   JAN 30 2015 9:29 PM

Did you fart, cause you blew me away.

✖ FYI, no one will be blowing you

Heyy did you fall from
the sky??

No, why?

This one better be good!

Cuz you look like a
dead bird

✖ No caption necessary

JACK MAR 6 2014 4:56 AM

Hey how are you? Quick question:
Greg, Sinead, Paul, Harry, and Jen are
trying to find seats at the cinema. Greg
must sit beside Sinead no matter what.
Jen cannot sit beside Harry. Paul must
sit on Jens right if Harry sits beside the
aisle. There must be one seat between
Jen and Harry. If Greg sits on the aisle,
will you sit on my face?

✘ If she says yes will you stop talking?

TIM JAN 6 2015 10:05 PM

On a scale of one to ten, how adorable
are mixed babies?

Like 10

Alright, I see. Now how many are you
looking for? I can supply however
many you want.

✘ Are you selling babies?

RYAN   JAN 26 2015 8:01 PM

One night with you is worth 18 years of child support

✖ Thankfully, we'll never find out

ANDRE   FEB 26 2015 1:52 AM

You look like a mix between MILEY and jesus.

Deeyum.

✖ She can twerk on water

PHILLIP   FEB 25 2015 11:00 PM

Damn girl, are you this pizza I just dropped on the floor because even though it's got some hair on it, I'm still gonna eat it

✖ 5-second rule applies

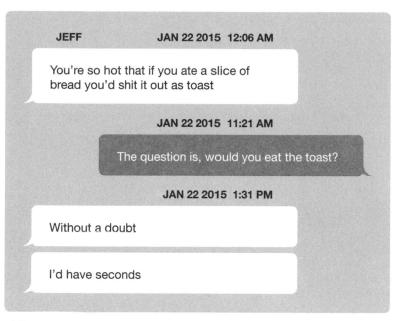

JEFF   JAN 22 2015 12:06 AM

You're so hot that if you ate a slice of bread you'd shit it out as toast

JAN 22 2015 11:21 AM

The question is, would you eat the toast?

JAN 22 2015 1:31 PM

Without a doubt

I'd have seconds

✖ I don't think that's how toast works

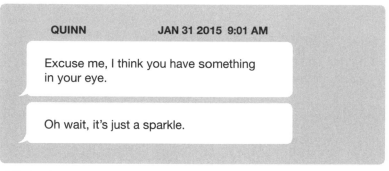

QUINN   JAN 31 2015 9:01 AM

Excuse me, I think you have something in your eye.

Oh wait, it's just a sparkle.

✖ Oh God

bad english

HEY U UP?

Nothing says romance quite like
someone who doesn't put any
effort whatsoever into getting in
your pants.

NO I'M NOT

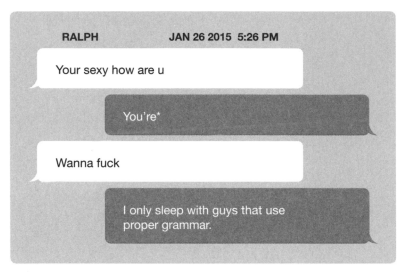

RALPH   JAN 26 2015 5:26 PM

Your sexy how are u

You're*

Wanna fuck

I only sleep with guys that use proper grammar.

✖ Your the worst

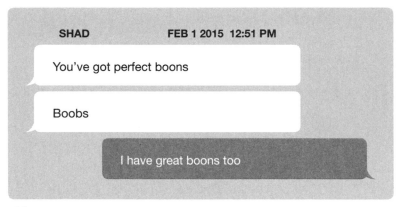

SHAD   FEB 1 2015 12:51 PM

You've got perfect boons

Boobs

I have great boons too

✖ I'm more of a lerg guy than a boon guy

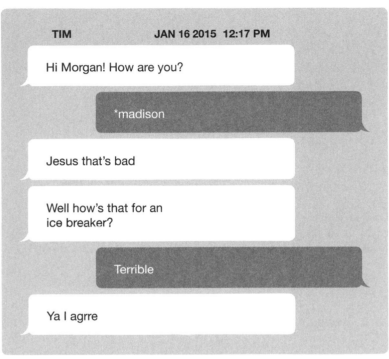

X Agree is spelled wrong. GET IT TOGETHER

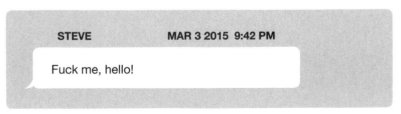

X Actually, it's pronounced Heather

JESSE   **JAN 31 2015 5:23 PM**

So here's what we do ,

I pick you , take you to a nice
fancy restaurant ... Candles ,
nice bottle of wine , free bread ,
fist you ...

You don't have to pay for any
of it if you don't want !!!

It all sounded great until you turned
into a tinder nightmare 👀

Fish stew "

I meant fish stew

Everyone loves fist you

Hahaha I think I'll pass thanks 👀😊

✖ Fish stew is equally as gross as this guy

I was going to call heaven and ask if you're an angle but I'm kind of hoping you're a slut.

Angle? I may be acute but don't know why you would call heaven for that....

✖ You're being obtuse

ADAM   MAR 2 2015 9:55 PM

Hello woman. I await you're response

Your

Fuck I blew it

✕ Yup

BRAD　　　　　JAN 9 2015 3:22 PM

Can we have sex in you're car

How about we don't do that and you learn how to use contractions correctly instead? 🤳

✖ The contraction you're looking for is: "We can't"

DAVE　　　　　JAN 25 2015 1:17 PM

Hi, how are you?

JAN 25 2015 4:02 PM

Would you be offended if I wanted to treat you about my sister, only different?

Something about that golf skirt makes me want to treat your corn hole like a coke bottle, blow on it, and make sweet, sweet music

✖ Wanted: A man that can treat me about my sister

STEPHEN   **JAN 22 2015 5:14 PM**

Your hot

JAN 23 2015 12:59 PM

You're*

✖ How many times do we have to go through this?

KEVIN JAN 14 2015 6:43 PM

What has 50 teeth and hold back a monster

No clue

My zipper

K

JAN 14 2015 10:35 PM

Your just a stuck up cunt aren't you

You're*

Smart to

Too*

What's the proper way to say fuck you

✖ Finally, he got something right!

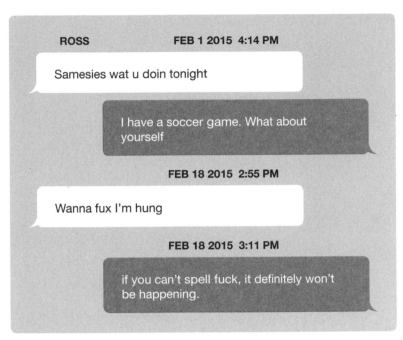

ROSS   FEB 1 2015 4:14 PM

Samesies wat u doin tonight

I have a soccer game. What about yourself

FEB 18 2015 2:55 PM

Wanna fux I'm hung

FEB 18 2015 3:11 PM

if you can't spell fuck, it definitely won't be happening.

✖ You can't even *spell* the thing you "wanna" do to her

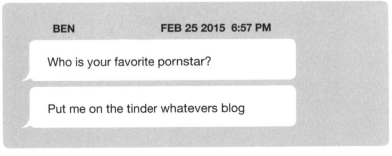

BEN   FEB 25 2015 6:57 PM

Who is your favorite pornstar?

Put me on the tinder whatevers blog

✖ Done and done

persistence

If at first you don't succeed,
try and try again. And then try
again. And then try again. Until
a restraining order is needed

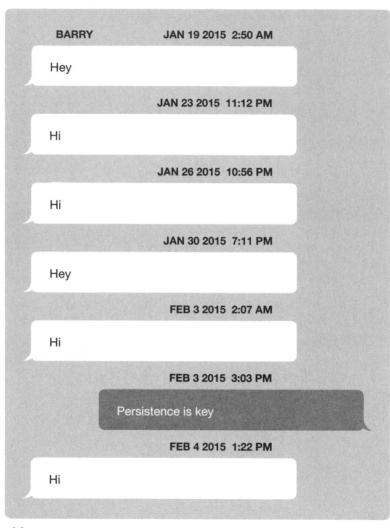

BARRY   JAN 19 2015 2:50 AM

Hey

JAN 23 2015 11:12 PM

Hi

JAN 26 2015 10:56 PM

Hi

JAN 30 2015 7:11 PM

Hey

FEB 3 2015 2:07 AM

Hi

FEB 3 2015 3:03 PM

Persistence is key

FEB 4 2015 1:22 PM

Hi

✖ No, *communication* is key

DAVE FEB 26 2015 8:38 PM

I drove past your house on the way to school and i was thinking about you and i was thinking about how beautiful you are and how lucky any guy is to date you because you are such a fun, caring and gorgeous girl. You are a girl a guy is proud to take home to meet his family, a girl that a guy is proud to show off to his friends and a girl a guy is glad to hang out with alone. You really have a great charm and you are absolutely beautiful :)

FEB 26 2015 9:22 PM

how do you know where I live? 😬

✖ Creepiness in full effect

EDDIE FEB 11 2015 6:14 PM

Hey there cutie:)

Did u really just add me on Facebook?

✖ ABORT

Between me and you
if we were in another
world and we forgot what
happened the other day

Will u sleep with me

Not necessary having sex

Like we have the chance
to be together right nos

✖ NO ONE knows what you're talking about

JAMES   JAN 28 2015 11:33 AM

You up for 2 minutes of mediocre sex
followed by 30 minutes of crying?

JAN 28 2015 1:54 PM

Judging by your hair you seem like a girl
who likes to do anal

JAN 28 2015 2:55 PM

Look I made a graph on how well this
conversation is going 📈

✖ Why are you crying? Is it because you're not funny?

BILL   FEB 8 2015 12:18 AM

Sexy

FEB 11 2015 9:22 PM

Still sexy

✖ Wow. Not much has changed in 3 days

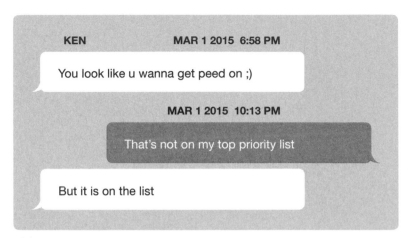

KEN   MAR 1 2015 6:58 PM

You look like u wanna get peed on ;)

MAR 1 2015 10:13 PM

That's not on my top priority list

But it is on the list

✘ Touché

MIKE   FEB 28 2015 2:28 PM

Beautiful

MAR 1 2015 9:15 PM

You could call me but don't respond lol?

MAR 2 2015 8:07 AM

Ok you stupid fuck don't click on me if you don't talk

✘ Their first date will be at an anger-management class

JEFF   **FEB 20 2015 4:11 PM**

We should have some hot
protected sex

FEB 23 2015 10:10 AM

Free this morning?

FEB 24 2015 3:16 PM

Free this afternoon?

FEB 25 2015 11:09 PM

I would love to go down
on you

FEB 26 2015 12:35 PM

Free today?

FEB 28 2015 9:58 AM

May I have your number?

✖ Backward everything did you

JOSH FEB 15 2015 4:45 PM

Are you still here?

FEB 16 2015 7:55 PM

Let me take you out for dinner

we obviously have a few things
to talk about

What's your favourite cuisine?

FEB 17 2015 2:17 PM

Oh well :(

FEB 18 2015 6:28 PM

You sure have a lot of cool shirts

FEB 19 2015 8:23 PM

Have you ever had a threesome?

✖ I bet she was just about to respond about the shirts too

NICK   JAN 26 2015 6:25 PM

Where're you from

JAN 26 2015 9:14 PM

We're obviously not
going to fuck then

How disappointing

✖ Sorry to let you down

JOHN   JAN 31 2015 9:11 AM

Hi

JAN 31 2015 11:26 AM

Hey hi how hows it going!?!?!

JAN 31 2015 11:43 AM

Are you gonna remove me ?

I have a big butt hole

✖ Just keep digging that grave

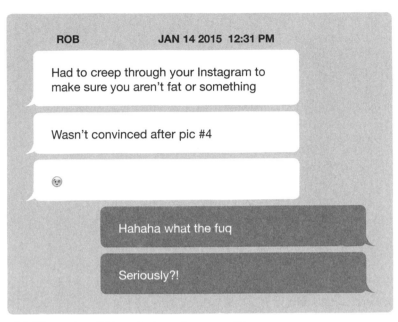

ROB　　　　　　JAN 14 2015 12:31 PM

Had to creep through your Instagram to make sure you aren't fat or something

Wasn't convinced after pic #4

😌

Hahaha what the fuq

Seriously?!

✖ File under: "Things to keep to yourself"

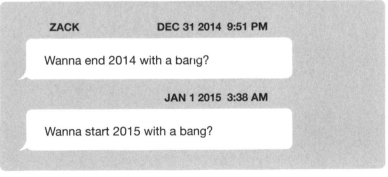

ZACK　　　　　DEC 31 2014 9:51 PM

Wanna end 2014 with a bang?

JAN 1 2015 3:38 AM

Wanna start 2015 with a bang?

✖ Points for consistency

SETH FEB 10 2015 1:55 PM

How much does a polar bear weigh?

FEB 11 2015 1:14 AM

How much

FEB 11 2015 7:49 AM

Enough to break the ice

FEB 12 2015 12:22 PM

Haha strike two

FEB 19 2015 9:33 AM

Anyway.

You're loss.

FEB 22 2015 8:37 PM

Can I lick your asshole

✖ You should have opened with that "can I lick your asshole" line

MICHELLE   FEB 25 2015 6:37 PM

handsome

{what are you looking for baby ? :-)|

|what are you looking for :-)
|what are you looking for?
|what are you looking for
|what are you looking for

ok id like to find someone for sex
is that weird :-)

Are you from the city?

i like weird things during sex how
about ? x

you can find my profile here
www.tinderprotect.com its a free
site that checks your over 18
and not a animal lol its for my safety

✘ This is either a pornbot or the weirdest woman alive

HIRO JAN 22 2015 6:15 PM

Lifes too short to beat around the bush hahaha

JAN 29 2015 8:52 PM

In my bluntest approach

I would like to fuck you

JAN 30 2015 1:14 AM

Alot of times

If that wouldnt be a problem my kind madam

Ahahhaa thats fucking cute

Cause im asian, and I will eat your cat

Hahahaha

✖ This just gets worse and worse every second

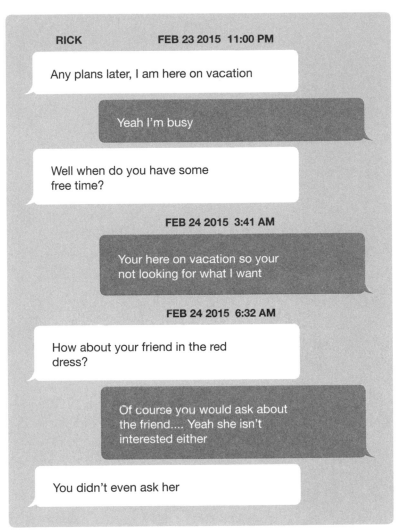

RICK FEB 23 2015 11:00 PM

Any plans later, I am here on vacation

Yeah I'm busy

Well when do you have some free time?

FEB 24 2015 3:41 AM

Your here on vacation so your not looking for what I want

FEB 24 2015 6:32 AM

How about your friend in the red dress?

Of course you would ask about the friend.... Yeah she isn't interested either

You didn't even ask her

✖ This guy needs a vacation from being alive

broetry

Always bad and seldom
smooth, when bros
write poetry, Shakespeare
spins in his grave

TOM   FEB 12 2015 6:09 PM

Roses are red violets are blue once a girl sat on my face I think you should to

 Too*

SHAUN   FEB 28 2015 2:19 PM

I would paddle across the Atlantic Ocean in a canoe made of hardened elephant foreskin with the Mexican soccer teams post game sweat as my water supply if it meant I could lace my shoes with your used dental floss...

Do less

✘ Simplicity at its finest

THEO   JAN 19 2015 1:13 AM

Your bio is as empty as my heart

✘ You seem like a blast!

ANDY   FEB 24 2015 2:11 PM

Roses are red
violets are fine
you be the
6 I'll be the 9

Does that ever actually work?

No but I'm not a quitter

✖ Never give up

JON   JAN 27 2015 7:03 PM

I know you might be scare of my age...
But hey let's move on to the next stage. I
am not a fake so when it's your birthday I
would to make you a cake.

It must be fate that we are a match, but
this is where the hatch began. If this is
fate then shall we go on a date?

✖ I'll have what he's having

MONTY   **MAR 2 2015 8:15 AM**

Roses are Red,
Violets are Blue,
We're a match on Here,
I think we should screw. :-)

 :-(

NICK   **FEB 19 2015 4:30 PM**

Roses are red, violets are blue. Do
you swallow like a good girl, or spit
like a prude?

✖ If you're going to be an asshole at least rhyme properly

KYLE   **JAN 31 2015 4:41 PM**

Roses r red
Violets r blue
Send me nudes and
maybe I'll fuck u

✖ Roses r red, clouds can b gray, I wish I had swiped the other way

Roses are red
violates are blue
you be the 6 and
I'll be the 9 ;)

✖ Great job, Alex. Just excellent work

EDWARD   MAR 2 2015 11:19 AM

I could have called heaven and asked for an angel but I'm hoping you're a slut instead.

✖ Heaven slut

BRAD   OCT 6 2014   10:23 AM

I've got candles, insence, and baby oil,
what have you got?

JAN 11 2015   1:47 PM

Your eyes are like a light house's gaze,
I'm trapped in the storm that is life and
then I see you, sweet relief.

✖ Sorry bro, your boat is capsizing

HUNTER   DEC 19 2014   7:21 PM

Roses are red
Violets are fine
You be the six
I'll be the nine

Roses are red,
violets are black.
I'd rather be buried alive
than go near your sack.

✖ Rap battle

TJ   MAR 2 2015 11:40 PM

Hey, I'm like chocolate pudding. i may look like shit but I'm as sweet as they come :)

✖ She'll definitely want to get to know you now!

MATT   FEB 15 2015 12:13 AM

Grass is green, so are your pants. I hate ants but I love federal grants.

FEB 15 2015 1:18 AM

Really?

✖ You stole this from Shakespeare, didn't you?

PETE   FEB 20 2015 7:50 PM

You make my wang as hard as a prosthetic leg

✖ Is that a simile or metaphor?

DOMINICK FEB 26 2015 11:25 AM

Are you toilet paper? Cuz I would let you touch my butt 🖤

Yikes....

✖ Romance is alive and two-ply

STEVE FEB 1 2015 2:49 AM

Roses are red panties are lace
I want you to sit on my face 😺 🎩

✖ Romantic and good at rhyming! What's not to love?

WILL MAR 2 2015 3:18 PM

You ever have one of those burps when all the food you've eaten in the past 4 hours comes flying out completely undigested?

✖ You mean throwing up? I'm doing that right now

booty calls

Let's skip the foreplay. Who cares about getting to know someone? Let's just cut to the chase and jam our jeans together

DAVID MAR 6 2015 2:53 AM

Do you want to have sex?

I promise it won't take long
I'll only be like two minutes!

✖ You're not making this any better

PAUL FEB 25 2015 1:57 PM

Listen. I'm not here to put boots
on caterpillars, do you want to
be sex friends?

✖ Putting tiny boots on caterpillars, now *that* would be impressive

VICTOR MAR 6 2015 10:09 PM

Mmmm mmmm, id like to lick maple
syrup off those cans.

✖ I'm telling my Aunt Jemima

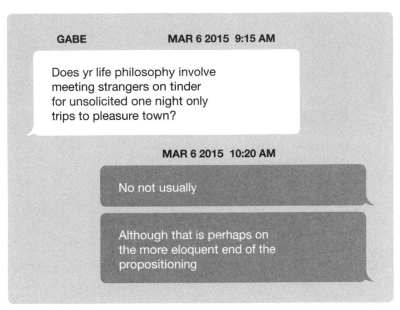

GABE   MAR 6 2015 9:15 AM

Does yr life philosophy involve meeting strangers on tinder for unsolicited one night only trips to pleasure town?

MAR 6 2015 10:20 AM

No not usually

Although that is perhaps on the more eloquent end of the propositioning

✖ Pleasure Town, Population: 0

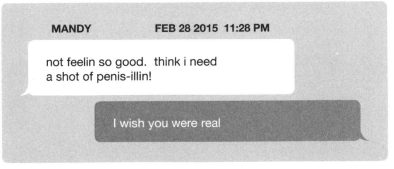

MANDY   FEB 28 2015 11:28 PM

not feelin so good. think i need a shot of penis-illin!

I wish you were real

✖ Mandy has chlamydia

PAT DEC 22 2014 12:08 AM

I wish I could take away all the chairs in the world so the only place for you to sit on would be my face 😌

But in all seriousness I bet you are a beautiful and a very interesting and intelligent woman

✖ Aww, you finished so strong!

MARK OCT 17 2014 9:07 PM

I have one serious question

and it's gonna sound like I'm a douche but I'm just getting it out of the way now rather than deal with it later....

Do you give head?

✖ He is 100 percent right: he sounds like a douche

ERIC — MAR 2 2015 8:53 PM

How many kids are we gonna have?

None I only do anal

So when's the wedding mommy?

✗ "So Mom, how did you meet Dad?"

BOB   FEB 8 2015 1:57 AM

Daises or Lillys?

FEB 11 2015 4:49 PM

Roses

FEB 11 2015 8:29 PM

Ahh ok

Just trying to figure out what
to put on the casket after i
murder that pussy

✘ Pro Tip: always work funerals into your pickup lines

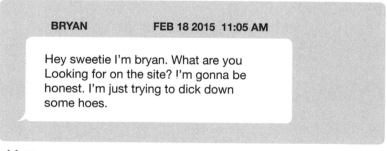

BRYAN   FEB 18 2015 11:05 AM

Hey sweetie I'm bryan. What are you
Looking for on the site? !'m gonna be
honest. I'm just trying to dick down
some hoes.

✘ Please don't call it "dicking down"

JENNY   FEB 26 2015 8:26 PM

Is my vagina crying or are you just sexy?

✗ You should probably see a doctor

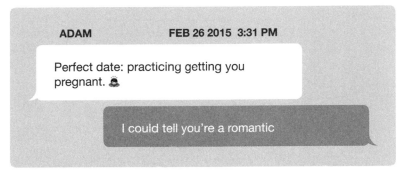

ADAM   FEB 26 2015 3:31 PM

Perfect date: practicing getting you pregnant. 🎂

I could tell you're a romantic

✗ You're giving me morning sickness

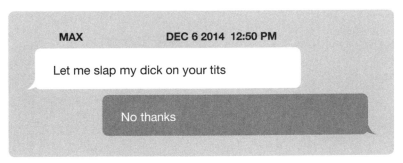

MAX   DEC 6 2014 12:50 PM

Let me slap my dick on your tits

No thanks

✗ But she really does appreciate your kind offer

strange requests

Just when you think you've
heard it all, you find out that
there are people out there who
have fetishes and desires your
mother did NOT warn you about

TOM   FEB 28 2015   8:12 PM

Wanna make some cash tonight?

✖ You're confusing Tinder with Craigslist

HAYDEN   JAN 16 2015   1:00 AM

Where do you live ?

JAN 16 2015   9:16 AM

How about a "hello" before you jump to a question like that.

✖ HELLO, WHERE DO YOU LIVE?

BRETT   NOV 17 2014   10:18 PM

It sure is cold out, mind if I use your thighs as earmuffs?

✖ Chill out, Brett

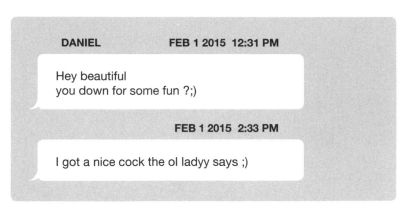

DANIEL   FEB 1 2015 12:31 PM

Hey beautiful
you down for some fun ?;)

FEB 1 2015 2:33 PM

I got a nice cock the ol ladyy says ;)

✖ Why are you showing old ladies your cock?

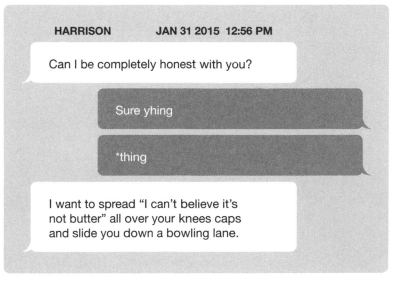

HARRISON   JAN 31 2015 12:56 PM

Can I be completely honest with you?

Sure yhing

*thing

I want to spread "I can't believe it's
not butter" all over your knees caps
and slide you down a bowling lane.

✖ Actually, this sounds fun

HOWIE   **JAN 26 2015 10:39 AM**

Hypothetically speaking...

if we were to move in together, what percentage of the house can I turn into a sex dungeon?

✖ All of it

BENJI   **JAN 26 2015 7:54 PM**

Would you be open to filling your ass with whip cream and farting it into my mouth? :-)

✖ Please die

JOHN   **JAN 8 2015 9:18 PM**

Hey yo girl do you squirt?

✖ Please. Just. Stop. Forever

Sometimes when I'm lonely, I go to the store. Then I buy all of the marinara sauce. Then I go home and fill up the bathtub. I slowly submerge myself into the sauce, and then curl up and pretend I'm a meatball.

Anyways, that's just a little bit about me. How are you?

✖ I'll never eat Italian again

Penis genitals

Really not the best way to say hello for the first time

Why not

How often are you nude around your family.

Have you ever heard of Tinder Nightmares?

✗ First of all, I am ALWAYS nude around my family

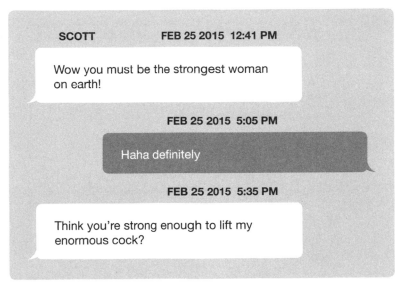

PETER   SEP 13 2014 11:42 PM

I came across your profile and I was enamored by your beauty. If I had the opportunity, I would take you on a date to Popeyes for some light appetizers. Then, I would bring you back to my place for some tv dinners, grape soda, and two hours straight of full house!

✖ You're more of a creepy uncle than a boyfriend

SCOTT   FEB 25 2015 12:41 PM

Wow you must be the strongest woman on earth!

FEB 25 2015 5:05 PM

Haha definitely

FEB 25 2015 5:35 PM

Think you're strong enough to lift my enormous cock?

✖ Yeah, she can probably lift 2 ounces

SIMON JAN 4 2015 8:12 PM

Can I make you my girlfriend so I can cum on your beautiful face?

 Your girlfriend is going to be one lucky lady!

DAVEY JAN 26 2015 4:55 PM

You and I are locked in a room for 24 hours.

I am wearing my Spartan costume and you cowgirl costume, complete with assless chaps.

We have 2 jars of grape jelly, a twister mat, a full shower with a detachable vibrating head, and the titanic sound track.

What happens next?

 Silence

ETHAN   JAN 9 2015 12:44 PM

I'm going to be 100% honest

I want to take you out to dinner (nowhere nice because I can't afford it) and then take you back to my place where we will watch a redbox movie (netflix is too expensive) after which we will hopefully engage in safe premarital sex.

Intercourse will most likely be somewhat disappointing and I may cry afterwards

but I promise that I will be both funny and charming the whole time!

✖ Get a job, sir

JONAS   JAN 16 2015 6:42 PM

Id love to suck your toes

✖ Let's start with a conversation, no?

Can I pee on you while you eat a ham sub?

FEB 22 2015 11:54 AM

Don't disrespect turkey subs by leaving them out like that.

FEB 22 2015 11:56 AM

What about pizza subs.

✗ I'm not horny but I *am* hungry

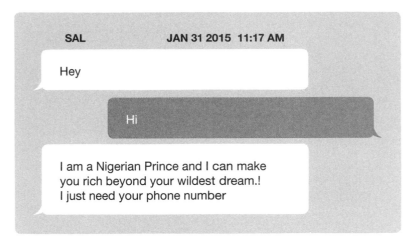

SAL   JAN 31 2015 11:17 AM

Hey

Hi

I am a Nigerian Prince and I can make you rich beyond your wildest dream.! I just need your phone number

✖ Would you like her social security number too?

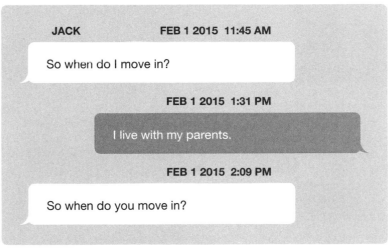

JACK   FEB 1 2015 11:45 AM

So when do I move in?

FEB 1 2015 1:31 PM

I live with my parents.

FEB 1 2015 2:09 PM

So when do you move in?

✖ It's like that tv show *Perfect Strangers*

JASON　　　FEB 14 2015　12:45 PM

So we could chat and I could try to charm you, or we could skip the BS, you could just come over, and we could hop in the shower... What do you say, life's too short to not let down your hair and enjoy things every once and awhile

Hahahaha. Nice attempt!!

How many times have you copied and pasted that in the chat box?

✖ You shouldn't waste water, Jason

JUSTIN　　　FEB 1 2015　1:15 PM

Hey how's it going?

Today I've realised that a shredded wheat on a stick makes a great back scrubber for the first couple of seconds of your bath. Just spreading the word x

✖ The more you know . . .

EDWARD   JAN 31 2015 8:38 PM

Half chicken half steak burrito bowl is the way to go

FEB 1 2015 9:32 AM

How many kids do you want?

How many eggs can be in your belly at once? A lot, probably.

✖ Do you just say everything you think?

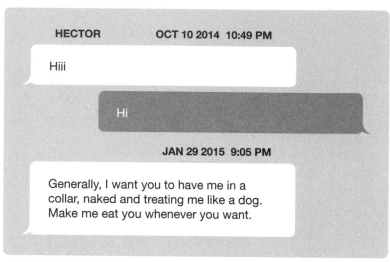

HECTOR **OCT 10 2014 10:49 PM**

Hiii

Hi

JAN 29 2015 9:05 PM

Generally, I want you to have me in a collar, naked and treating me like a dog. Make me eat you whenever you want.

✖ Don't let the doggy door hit you on the way out

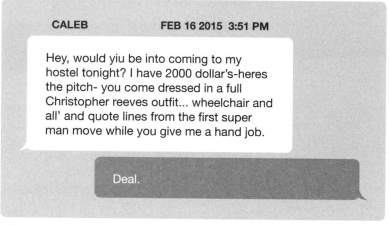

CALEB **FEB 16 2015 3:51 PM**

Hey, would yiu be into coming to my hostel tonight? I have 2000 dollar's-heres the pitch- you come dressed in a full Christopher reeves outfit... wheelchair and all' and quote lines from the first super man move while you give me a hand job.

Deal.

✖ I would take this deal too

BRIAN JAN 24 2015 2:34 PM

Let's snort a mountain of molly and casually finger paint each others naked bodies, before watching Netflix until my account expires.

And in the morning I'd cook you breakfast.

Great offer, I'm in

Well first we have to test your finger paint abilities

I don't want lame art on me you know?

✖ Renew your account and we'll talk

NOAH NOV 1 2014 3:17 AM

What is your bmi?

✖ Her BMI is GFY

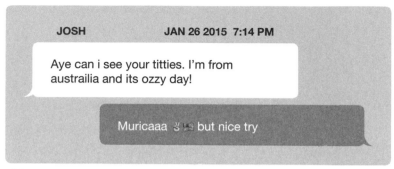

JOSH   JAN 26 2015 7:14 PM

Aye can i see your titties. I'm from austrailia and its ozzy day!

Muricaaa 🌿🇺🇸 but nice try

✖ You must be the ambassador

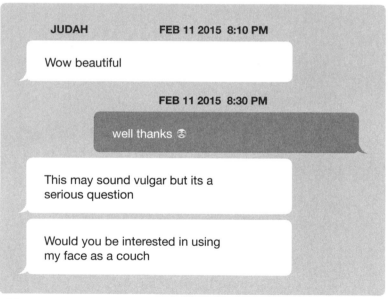

JUDAH   FEB 11 2015 8:10 PM

Wow beautiful

FEB 11 2015 8:30 PM

well thanks 😳

This may sound vulgar but its a serious question

Would you be interested in using my face as a couch

✖ Sounds more like a loveseat than a couch

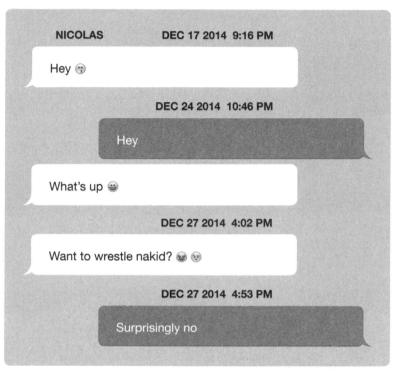

NICOLAS DEC 17 2014 9:16 PM

Hey

DEC 24 2014 10:46 PM

Hey

What's up

DEC 27 2014 4:02 PM

Want to wrestle nakid?

DEC 27 2014 4:53 PM

Surprisingly no

✖ Na, kid

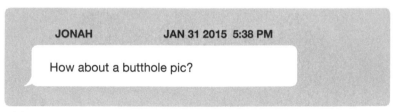

JONAH JAN 31 2015 5:38 PM

How about a butthole pic?

✖ She's looking at one now

shot down

Like hitting a home run out of
the park, there are few feelings
more wonderful than taking a
creep down a few pegs

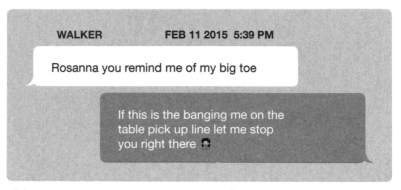

WALKER　　　　**FEB 11 2015 5:39 PM**

Rosanna you remind me of my big toe

If this is the banging me on the table pick up line let me stop you right there 💀

✖ NAILED IT

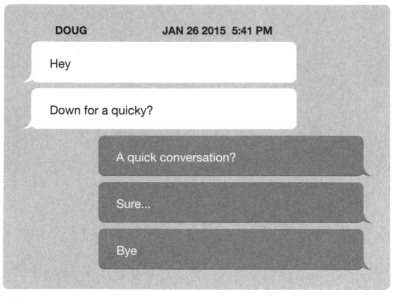

DOUG　　　　**JAN 26 2015 5:41 PM**

Hey

Down for a quicky?

A quick conversation?

Sure...

Bye

✖ That was fast!

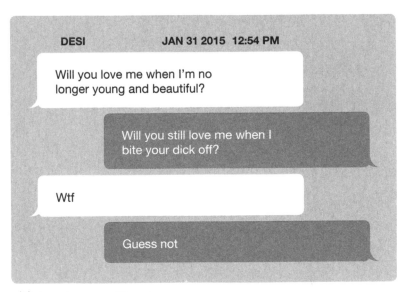

DESI JAN 31 2015 12:54 PM

Will you love me when I'm no longer young and beautiful?

Will you still love me when I bite your dick off?

Wtf

Guess not

✖ Love is unconditional

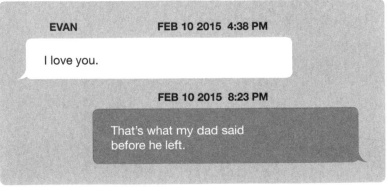

EVAN FEB 10 2015 4:38 PM

I love you.

FEB 10 2015 8:23 PM

That's what my dad said before he left.

✖ Buzzkill

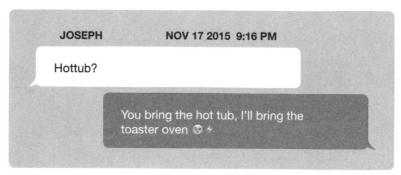

JOSEPH   **NOV 17 2015 9:16 PM**

Hottub?

You bring the hot tub, I'll bring the toaster oven 😌 ⚡

✖ How does one "bring" a hot tub?

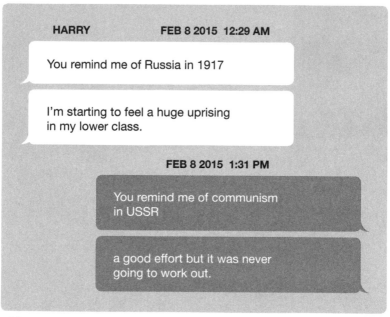

HARRY   **FEB 8 2015 12:29 AM**

You remind me of Russia in 1917

I'm starting to feel a huge uprising in my lower class.

FEB 8 2015 1:31 PM

You remind me of communism in USSR

a good effort but it was never going to work out.

✖ Sadly, these two people are probably meant to be

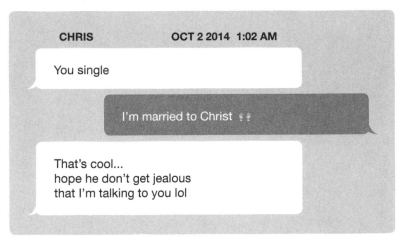

CHRIS   **OCT 2 2014 1:02 AM**

You single

I'm married to Christ 🙏

That's cool...
hope he don't get jealous
that I'm talking to you lol

✖ That's his cross to bear

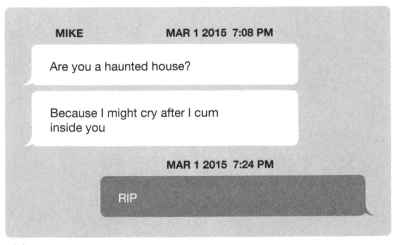

MIKE   **MAR 1 2015 7:08 PM**

Are you a haunted house?

Because I might cry after I cum
inside you

MAR 1 2015 7:24 PM

RIP

✖ Now that's what I call an O-bitch-uary

CRAIG MAR 8 2015 3:13 AM

Hey lover what u up to

MAR 8 2015 5:48 AM

Wanna meet up?

MAR 8 2015 10:16 AM

Nah

MAR 8 2015 1:00 PM

Me neither

✖ LIES

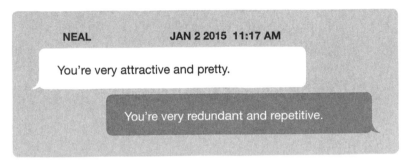

NEAL JAN 2 2015 11:17 AM

You're very attractive and pretty.

You're very redundant and repetitive.

✖ Take the fucking compliment

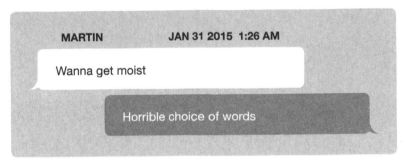

MARTIN JAN 31 2015 1:26 AM

Wanna get moist

Horrible choice of words

✖ I prefer damp

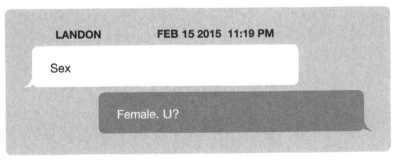

LANDON FEB 15 2015 11:19 PM

Sex

Female. U?

✖ No, see, what he meant was . . .

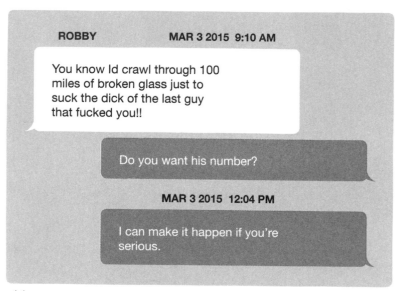

ROBBY   MAR 3 2015 9:10 AM

You know Id crawl through 100 miles of broken glass just to suck the dick of the last guy that fucked you!!

Do you want his number?

MAR 3 2015 12:04 PM

I can make it happen if you're serious.

✖ Next season on *Fear Factor* . . .

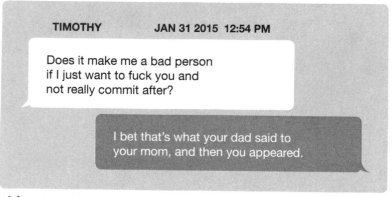

TIMOTHY   JAN 31 2015 12:54 PM

Does it make me a bad person if I just want to fuck you and not really commit after?

I bet that's what your dad said to your mom, and then you appeared.

✖ It doesn't make you a bad person. It just ends this conversation

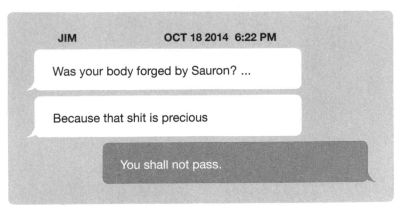

JIM　　　　　　　　**OCT 18 2014　6:22 PM**

Was your body forged by Sauron? ...

Because that shit is precious

You shall not pass.

✖ More like *Lord of the Wrongs*

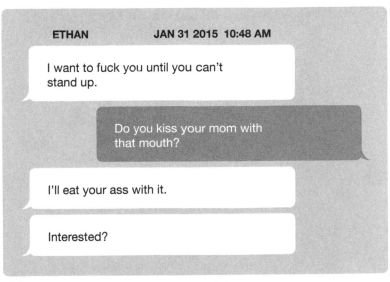

ETHAN　　　　　　**JAN 31 2015　10:48 AM**

I want to fuck you until you can't stand up.

Do you kiss your mom with that mouth?

I'll eat your ass with it.

Interested?

✖ But will he pay for your therapy bills?

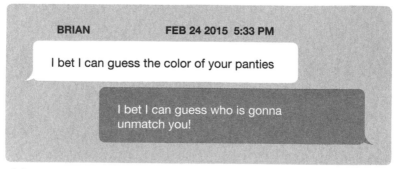

BRIAN   FEB 24 2015 5:33 PM

I bet I can guess the color of your panties

I bet I can guess who is gonna unmatch you!

✖ Well to be fair, that's not really a guess

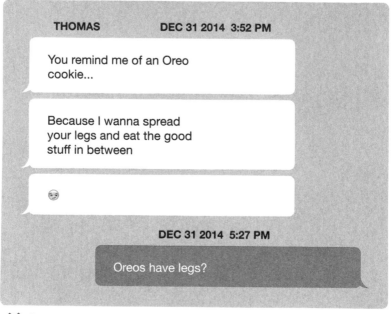

THOMAS   DEC 31 2014 3:52 PM

You remind me of an Oreo cookie...

Because I wanna spread your legs and eat the good stuff in between

😊

DEC 31 2014 5:27 PM

Oreos have legs?

✖ Anatomy of a cookie

KURT MAR 1 2015 11:27 PM

In the words of an terrible pop band of the 1990s: 'I wanna sex you up.'

In the words of an awesome pop rapper of the 1990s: "You can't touch this."

✗ He's 2 Legit 2 Quit

JACOB JAN 24 2015 9:45 PM

Did you know that romeo and juliets romance was only 1 week long?

JAN 26 2015 8:22 PM

Did you know that it also ended in a gruesome double-suicide?

✗ That's less romantic than how I remember it

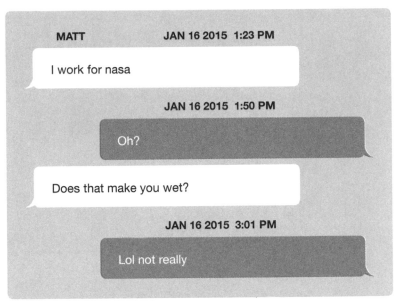

MATT JAN 16 2015 1:23 PM

I work for nasa

JAN 16 2015 1:50 PM

Oh?

Does that make you wet?

JAN 16 2015 3:01 PM

Lol not really

✖ I need space

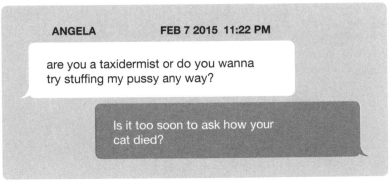

ANGELA FEB 7 2015 11:22 PM

are you a taxidermist or do you wanna try stuffing my pussy any way?

Is it too soon to ask how your cat died?

✖ We loved Fluffy

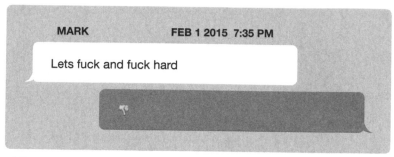

MARK　　　　　FEB 1 2015　7:35 PM

Lets fuck and fuck hard

✖ Let's not and not hard

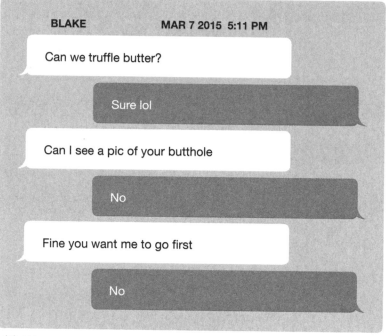

BLAKE　　　　　MAR 7 2015　5:11 PM

Can we truffle butter?

Sure lol

Can I see a pic of your butthole

No

Fine you want me to go first

No

✖ What. Is. Truffle. Butter

HENRY MAR 5 2015 5:20 PM

Will you ride me like the guy in pic #3?

MAR 5 2015 8:42 PM

Well considering that's a picture of me and my 92 year old grandpa I'm going to have to pass.

✗ I really want to see this picture

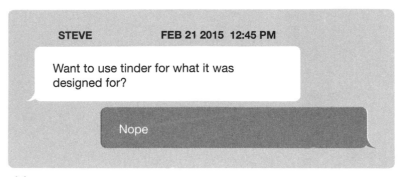

STEVE   FEB 21 2015 12:45 PM

Want to use tinder for what it was designed for?

Nope

✖ To light something on fire???

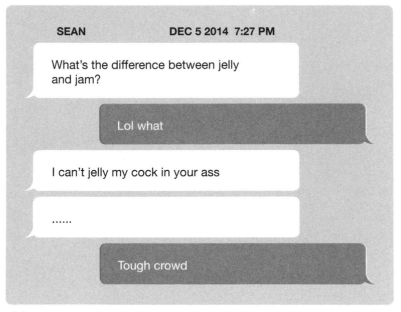

SEAN   DEC 5 2014 7:27 PM

What's the difference between jelly and jam?

Lol what

I can't jelly my cock in your ass

......

Tough crowd

✖ Nothing can preserve this relationship

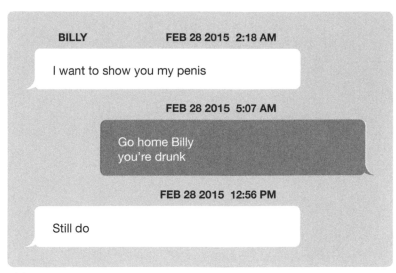

BILLY FEB 28 2015 2:18 AM

I want to show you my penis

FEB 28 2015 5:07 AM

Go home Billy
you're drunk

FEB 28 2015 12:56 PM

Still do

✖ Billy is committed

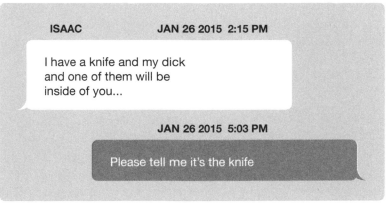

ISAAC JAN 26 2015 2:15 PM

I have a knife and my dick
and one of them will be
inside of you...

JAN 26 2015 5:03 PM

Please tell me it's the knife

✖ Sophie's choice

sneak attacks

You're having a nice conversation. You think you've met a charming person, and then, like a cobra uncoiling, the freaks are out! Your defenses are useless!

This is a sneak attack

LARRY DEC 23 2014 7:20 AM

Marry me?!

DEC 23 2014 3:52 PM

Dinner First?

DEC 23 2014 6:22 PM

Lol sure thing!

How's tinder treating you?!

Where about's do you live?

DEC 30 2014 11:30 PM

You alive?

FEB 20 2015 4:15 PM

God
I want to be inside you

✖ Even God is embarrassed by this conversation

ELIJAH MAR 2 2015 3:56 PM

Ashley how are you? What brings you to tinder?

MAR 2 2015 5:04 PM

Do you enjoy anal sex?

✖ A+ material here

BEN FEB 1 2015 12:14 PM

Hi Zoe, I just wanted to know what you want from Tinder...

FEB 1 2015 2:22 PM

Hey, I'm looking for a potential boyfriend to be fair. What about you?

FEB 1 2015 3:11 PM

I'm looking to be balls deep in vagina :)

✖ The smiley face really makes everything ok

LYLE JAN 16 2015 5:08 PM

Im gonna make you moan like a harpooned whale.

✖ Well that's horrifying

BLAINE APR 4 2014 1:54 PM

I want to bend you over the kitchen counter and slide into you from behind and slam into you until you scream

I mean hi

✖ Reverse the order

JOE FEB 9 2015 12:08 AM

Hii
Please be kinky

✖ At least he said please

Do you like whales?

I'm a huge fan of whales. Definitely

Great! Because we can humpback at my place

✖ We dolphinately won't be doing that

SIMON DEC 9 2014 8:37 PM

Would you like to come over this weekend and get close?

I would love to!

How do you feel about chlamydia?

Gross. What?

Well you said you wanted to get close so I just needed your opinion on chlamydia.

That's weird.

Not sure if I wanna get close now.

Ok so no to chlamydia. Well how do you feel about strap ons?

✖ Oh, they're going to get really close, really fast

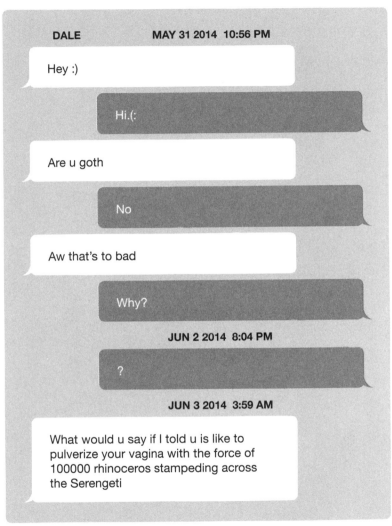

DALE   MAY 31 2014 10:56 PM

Hey :)

Hi.(:

Are u goth

No

Aw that's to bad

Why?

JUN 2 2014 8:04 PM

?

JUN 3 2014 3:59 AM

What would u say if I told u is like to pulverize your vagina with the force of 100000 rhinoceros stampeding across the Serengeti

✘ Because everyone knows goth kids love African safaris

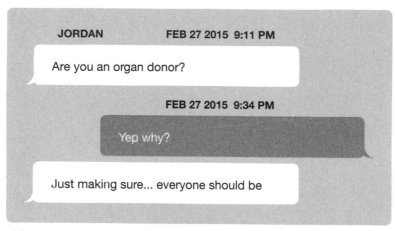

JORDAN FEB 27 2015 9:11 PM

Are you an organ donor?

FEB 27 2015 9:34 PM

Yep why?

Just making sure... everyone should be

✖ I thought this was going somewhere else entirely

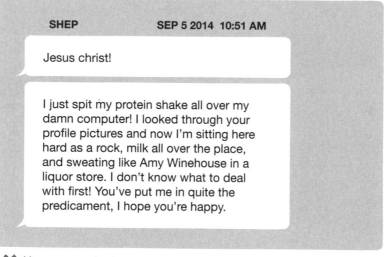

SHEP SEP 5 2014 10:51 AM

Jesus christ!

I just spit my protein shake all over my damn computer! I looked through your profile pictures and now I'm sitting here hard as a rock, milk all over the place, and sweating like Amy Winehouse in a liquor store. I don't know what to deal with first! You've put me in quite the predicament, I hope you're happy.

✖ How are you looking at Tinder on your computer?

JAKE   FEB 22 2015 1:52 PM

Beard game on point 🫳

FEB 22 2015 2:16 PM

Thank you!

FEB 22 2015 2:17 PM

Great chatting...

FEB 22 2015 3:03 PM

Anal

✖ WHAT THE FUCK IS WRONG WITH YOU PEOPLE

Hey, are you an archaeologist by chance?

Lol no...

Shame, bc I have a large bone that needs examining

✘ This relationship is about to be extinct

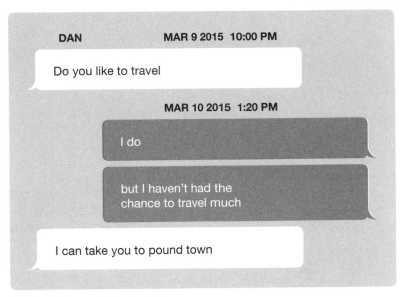

✘ Is that near Cleveland?

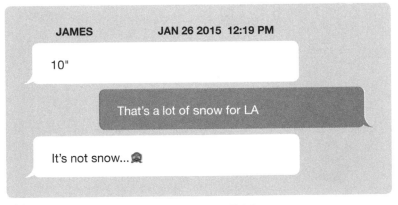

✘ Did you blind the monkey with your dick?

IAN FEB 1 2015 1:48 AM

You have beautiful eyes!

Well thank you

What does your brown eye look like

I'm sorry

that was incredibly forward of me

That probably made you think I'm some freak and scared you off

You don't think im a freak do you?

Great now im nervous

✖ How did everything go so wrong?

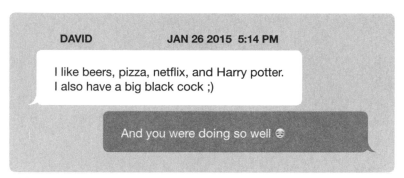

DAVID   JAN 26 2015 5:14 PM

I like beers, pizza, netflix, and Harry potter.
I also have a big black cock ;)

And you were doing so well 😔

✖ Were you born on a farm? Do you think this is how dating works?

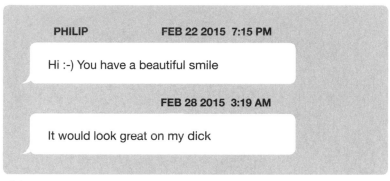

PHILIP   FEB 22 2015 7:15 PM

Hi :-) You have a beautiful smile

FEB 28 2015 3:19 AM

It would look great on my dick

✖ What's nicer than a dicksmile?

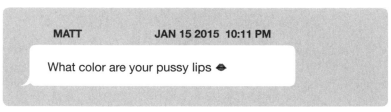

MATT   JAN 15 2015 10:11 PM

What color are your pussy lips 👄

✖ Red. Like a stop sign

KYLE FEB 26 2015 9:35 PM

How good can you cook breakfast? I have a thing for big girls with big foreheads and if we do this I don't wanna be disappointed in the morning

1. I'm a fantastic cook thank you very much. 2. I didn't realize I had a big forehead? Or that foreheads are even a thing? 3. I'm not here for one night stands so sorry not sorry buddy.

So no butt stuff?

✖ No, Kyle, no butt stuff

JEFF JAN 31 2015 8:26 PM

Hey

I'm really good at beating off. Terrible at sex. Just thought you should know

✖ I think she was was about to say "hey" but you ruined everything

Hey how are you?

Fine you?

Good!

Lovely

Maybe a little horny

✌️

✖ I'm guessing more than a little!

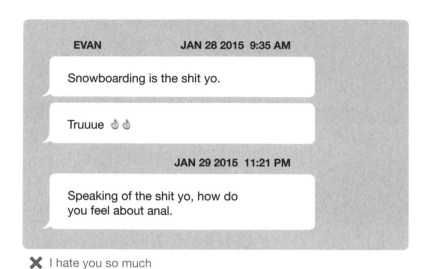

EVAN   JAN 28 2015   9:35 AM

Snowboarding is the shit yo.

Truuue 👌👌

JAN 29 2015   11:21 PM

Speaking of the shit yo, how do you feel about anal.

✖ I hate you so much

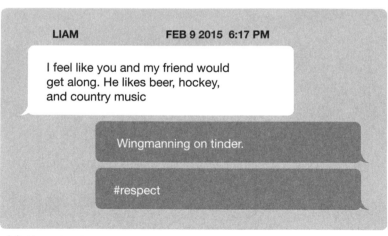

LIAM   FEB 9 2015   6:17 PM

I feel like you and my friend would get along. He likes beer, hockey, and country music

Wingmanning on tinder.

#respect

✖ Not what I expected

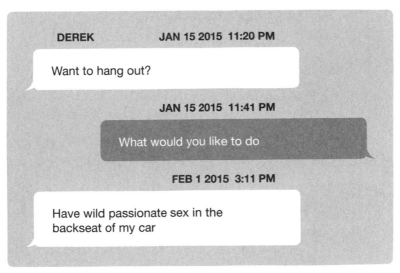

✖ "Passionate sex" and "backseat" don't belong together

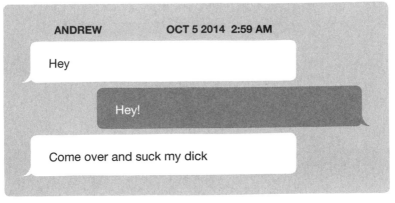

✖ Oh, okay! . . . Wait a minute . . . no!

MIKE   JAN 26 2015 9:09 PM

I want to raw dog you

JAN 26 2015 9:43 PM

✖ Woof

BRIAN   FEB 23 2015 1:16 PM

I just wanna buy you chipotle and call you beautiful 😔

Alright ill just go fist my self

and I'll throw tacos at you when I see you

✖ WHAT!?

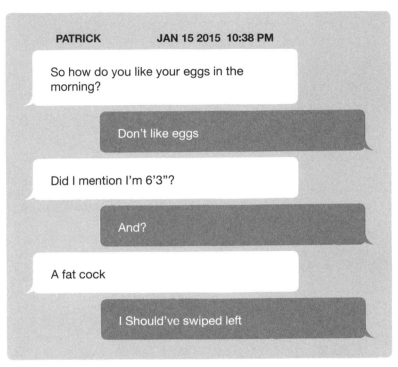

PATRICK JAN 15 2015 10:38 PM

So how do you like your eggs in the morning?

Don't like eggs

Did I mention I'm 6'3"?

And?

A fat cock

I Should've swiped left

✖ That's disgusting, who doesn't like eggs?

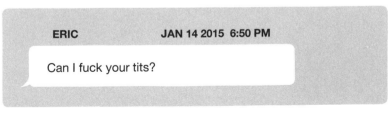

ERIC JAN 14 2015 6:50 PM

Can I fuck your tits?

✖ No. Just, no

random weirdness

Some things in life just don't make sense. These are those things

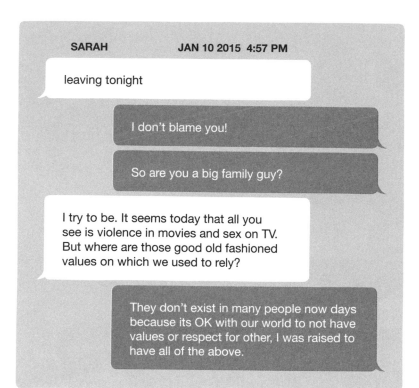

SARAH   JAN 10 2015 4:57 PM

leaving tonight

I don't blame you!

So are you a big family guy?

I try to be. It seems today that all you see is violence in movies and sex on TV. But where are those good old fashioned values on which we used to rely?

They don't exist in many people now days because its OK with our world to not have values or respect for other, I was raised to have all of the above.

✖ Lucky there's a *Family Guy*!

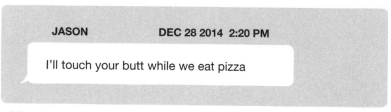

JASON   DEC 28 2014 2:20 PM

I'll touch your butt while we eat pizza

✖ No, actually, you won't

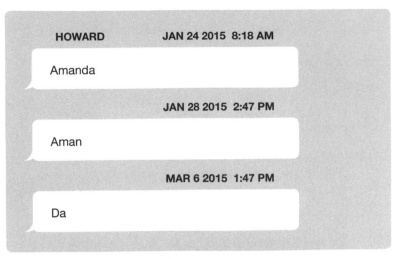

HOWARD   **JAN 24 2015 8:18 AM**

Amanda

JAN 28 2015 2:47 PM

Aman

MAR 6 2015 1:47 PM

Da

✖ Tho 5-week gap is super impressive

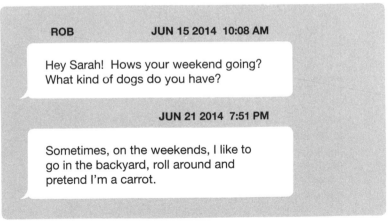

ROB   **JUN 15 2014 10:08 AM**

Hey Sarah! Hows your weekend going? What kind of dogs do you have?

JUN 21 2014 7:51 PM

Sometimes, on the weekends, I like to go in the backyard, roll around and pretend I'm a carrot.

✖ Never let this guy dog-sit

TOM JAN 26 2015 12:38 AM

is it normal to cry during sex

asking for a friend

no it's not

oh

i don't have friends btw

✖ You seem balanced

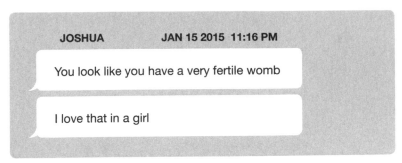

JOSHUA   JAN 15 2015 11:16 PM

You look like you have a very fertile womb

I love that in a girl

✖ A womb belongs in a girl

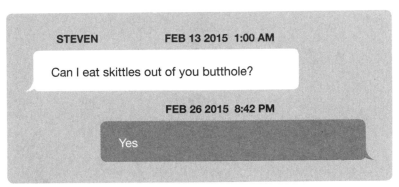

STEVEN   FEB 13 2015 1:00 AM

Can I eat skittles out of you butthole?

FEB 26 2015 8:42 PM

Yes

✖ Taste the rainbow

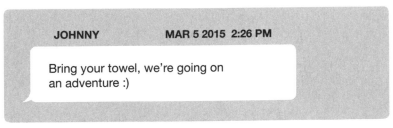

JOHNNY   MAR 5 2015 2:26 PM

Bring your towel, we're going on an adventure :)

✖ One-way ticket to FuckOffLand

BLAINE   FEB 1 2015 6:54 PM

Hey, you pretty hot. I'm gonna lay my cards out on the table and be straight from the go. I've very recently come out of a 4 year relationship and to be honest it's still a little raw. So I'm not really looking for my next missus just yet, in fact, I'm not really sure what I'm looking for or why I'm even on here.... I guess I'm probably looking for someone to suck the remaining broken fragments of my soul out of my body......

through my cock 😉

are you that saviour? X

✖ Douchebag 3:16

ALEX   JAN 31 2015 9:43 PM

Hey there. I once farted so bad my cat had a seizure.

✖ How are you still single?

SHANE   FEB 22 2015   4:26 PM

If you were a marshmallow, I'd fluff you good

✖ I think you mean pillow?

HARRIS   JAN 31 2015   1:25 AM

If I was a hippo I would fight off every other male hippo to protect you!

I would be the hippo king and i would make you my hippo queen and we could rule the African puddles together!

✖ I think I'm in love

MATTHEW   FEB 1 2015   9:58 PM

Hey Kali, do you live in a cornfield? Bc I'm stalking you

✖ You're pretty corny yourself there, bro . . .

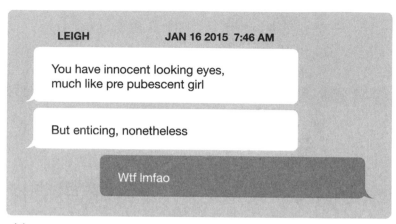

LEIGH JAN 16 2015 7:46 AM

You have innocent looking eyes, much like pre pubescent girl

But enticing, nonetheless

Wtf lmfao

✖ Shouldn't you be on a list somewhere?

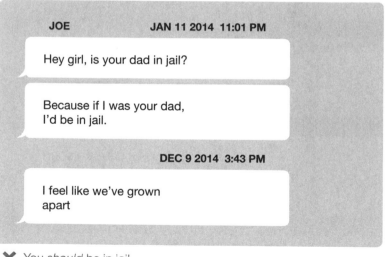

JOE JAN 11 2014 11:01 PM

Hey girl, is your dad in jail?

Because if I was your dad, I'd be in jail.

DEC 9 2014 3:43 PM

I feel like we've grown apart

✖ You *should* be in jail

ZACH   FEB 25 2015 11:27 PM

i have a top hat that
fits my penis

Impressive

Jk fucking got you

it's a cowboy hat

✖ JK, it's a thimble

JOE MAR 2 2015 8:07 PM

I like the shape of your head

Thanks?

Haha It's a compliment...

✖ Bone structure is crucial

RAY　　　　JAN 31 2015　8:32 PM

Wow. If you ever get mauled by a polar bear with chainsaw hands, I hope he stays away from your face...

Because I think you're cute

 I actually *would* date this man

BOB　　　　FEB 26 2015　4:57 PM

Hi.

I have a vagina.

 Sold!

CHRIS　　　　NOV 8 2014　8:46 PM

So, you look like you have a healthy coke habit.

 Insult? Compliment?

JAKE DEC 24 2014 11:04 AM

I once ate a full block of cheese for $20, hard times...

Hahaha!
Why are you telling me this?

I actually started making money by doing it. I'd eat all sorts of heavy shit, drew the line at a cup of Crisco for $50 though. Couldn't push myself through it. I Guess I'm just displaying the hardships of my childhood ... Might be a way of courting?

Is this your way of telling me I'll have to pay for dinner?

✖ Man vs. Food vs. Common Sense

SEAN DEC 30 2014 6:46 PM

Is your sister single?

ELISE JAN 31 2015 10:47 PM

You make me wish I had a penis

✖ You make me wish I didn't

FRED MAR 12 2015 11:00 AM

Girl I would pick you up in my 01 Chevy Malibu, take you to Taco Bell, and let you get that crunch wrap baby. We both lock eyes as we takes gulps out of our 42 oz baja blasts instantly falling head over heals for each other. The moment is so perfect I'd get on one knee right there and propose to you via a mild hot sauce packet. After I'd take you straight to the nearest liquor store to buy the cheapest box wine I could find. Then we go to my place, get comfortable, pour that room temperature wine in some styrofoam cups, and just let you watch whatever you want on Netflix before my neighbors catch me using their account again.

✖ I died of boredom twice while reading this

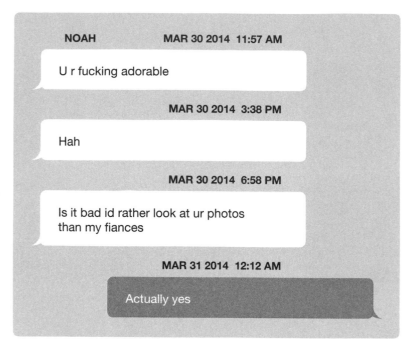

NOAH   MAR 30 2014 11:57 AM

U r fucking adorable

MAR 30 2014 3:38 PM

Hah

MAR 30 2014 6:58 PM

Is it bad id rather look at ur photos than my fiances

MAR 31 2014 12:12 AM

Actually yes

✖ Yeah, it's bad. It makes you one of the worst people on Earth

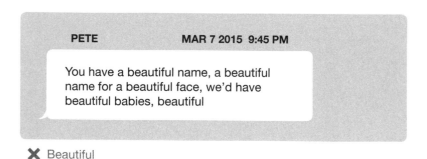

PETE   MAR 7 2015 9:45 PM

You have a beautiful name, a beautiful name for a beautiful face, we'd have beautiful babies, beautiful

✖ Beautiful

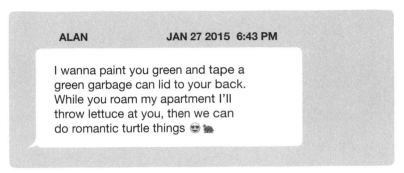

ALAN   JAN 27 2015 6:43 PM

I wanna paint you green and tape a green garbage can lid to your back. While you roam my apartment I'll throw lettuce at you, then we can do romantic turtle things 😍 🐢

✖ Ever heard of dinner and a movie?

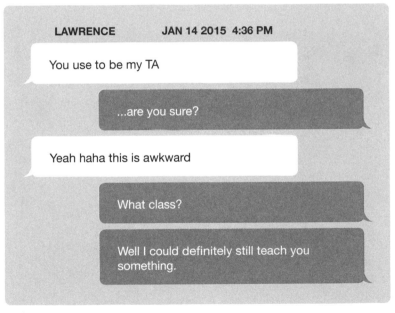

LAWRENCE   JAN 14 2015 4:36 PM

You use to be my TA

...are you sure?

Yeah haha this is awkward

What class?

Well I could definitely still teach you something.

✖ Why don't you stay after class?

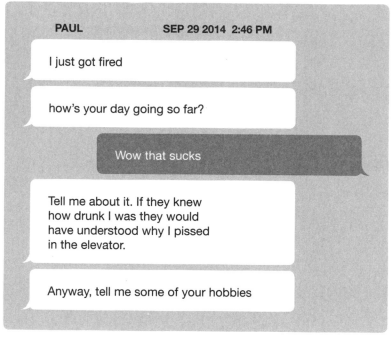

ERIC   **JAN 22 2015 6:14 PM**

On a scale of 0-10 how much do you want to show me your butt hole?

✖ Is there a negative scale here somewhere?

PAUL   **SEP 29 2014 2:46 PM**

I just got fired

how's your day going so far?

Wow that sucks

Tell me about it. If they knew how drunk I was they would have understood why I pissed in the elevator.

Anyway, tell me some of your hobbies

✖ My hobbies include slowly backing away from you

NATHAN **JUL 18 2013 1:20 AM**

Hey there :)

JUL 23 2013 2:59 AM

You know we're cousins right? Lol
Btw how the hell did you match
me in Israel?

✖ WHY DID YOU SWIPE RIGHT?

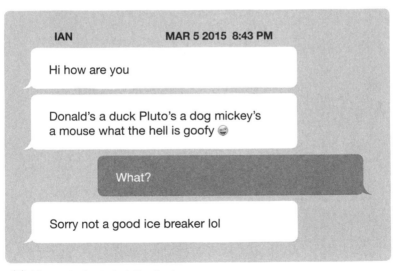

IAN **MAR 5 2015 8:43 PM**

Hi how are you

Donald's a duck Pluto's a dog mickey's
a mouse what the hell is goofy 😂

What?

Sorry not a good ice breaker lol

✖ Honestly, just shut the fuck up

ZACK **JAN 19 2015 11:30 AM**

Hey how's your
weekend going?

JAN 28 2015 12:01 PM

We would've had
beautiful babies

✖ No, you wouldn't have

BRENDAN   JAN 31 2015 10:46 PM

Im kidding of course. but seriously, let me tell you a little about myself. It all started when three friends and I, sparked by curiosity, set out on an adventure to go looking for a body of a kid who went missing. We were followed closely by some older bad kids who wanted to take credit for finding the dead kid. Looking back, we had a variety rose-tinted behavioral adolescent experiences that defined our pre-pubescent personalities and foreshowed who we would become. Once we found the body the bad kids caught up to us. One of them had a gun but I got ahold of it and.... wait, that was Stand by Me. I'm a graphic designer.

haha, no response to that

✖ No one has time to read this

SCOTT   FEB 1 2015 11:09 AM

I'd put hot sauce on you

✖ Sounds uncomfortable

JORDAN   FEB 28 2015 3:26 PM

I just sold a Viagra to a college kid after convincing him it's Adderall.

He's going to have a very hard test tomorrow.

✖ Cool felony, bro

JOE   NOV 28 2014 12:03 PM

Hey there 😊
What part of Ethiopia are you form?

NOV 28 2014 11:10 PM

I'm from Texas...

NOV 29 2014 5:00 PM

Oh right on! You look Ethiopian. Take it as a complement, Ethiopian women are very beautiful. What part of TX are you from?

✖ Joe's not great with geography

slowly massage the vag, then rub the clitoris ever so gently. Proceed to stick a single finger in the vagina. continue adding your fingers until your whole fist is in. slide your arm slowly into her, once you reach your shoulder limbo in with your head, and forcibly insert your other arm, torso, and legs. You are now free to control her. when you feel the job is done, finish by giving birth to yourself

✖ There is literally nothing to say about this

acknowledgments

Unspirational would like to thank the following people for the following vague and terrifying reasons:

Elan Gale. Your fearless leadership, bitter cynicism, and limitless anger have been a constant source of unspiration. Everything is right in this horrible, horrible world.

Bill Dixon. Thank you for your tireless commitment to bring more sadness to the masses. Laughter follows.

Heather Pasternak. The ship only floats when the plans are sublime. Namaste.

Matt Wise. It is not enough to see a tree in a forest. One must burn down all the other trees to make sure you're tapping the sap of the right one. Spread the fuel everywhere. Fire.

Samantha Weiner. The future is vast and desolate and bleak and that makes all things possible.

David Fox. No better name can even.

Furthermore, the following series of glyphs and acronyms indicate gratitude towards our legions of quiet and brave contributors

Dark Clan TTG / TBG / SJG / GMDB calC kraD ehT

Army Of Silence MMW / ADR / PM / MLM / PJS / CEL / JPR / JG / Insert name (YALBMYSMF)

Ysor Battalion CBH / MH / MF / RM / AR / NW / SJF / BG / Insert name

Triad SH / SL / CG / KB / WB / AD / NF / BT / COB / AI / JLR / CW / DK / CBR / AH / EGM / JH / BF / AL / TM / CW / BH / CC / AF / Insert Name / PM / MM / SC / AB / TA / Forgotten and Fallen / XX / NV / LS

Jac, Liz, Remington, Betches, Shira, Jenny, Christy, Mandy, Travon

Shrouded and swirling forces at Foundry, CAA, and Abrams

EVERYTHING IS BAD. SOME THINGS ARE WORSE.

WE ARE HERE TO HELP.